Here's to big dogs and all their little shenanigans!

Special thanks to Erin for sharing her love of Milly and making me a Great Dane aunt. Also, thanks to Ilona, Sandy, and Marty for all they do.

Follow Silly Milly on Instagram @sillymillythedane

Also available in Milly's silly collection:

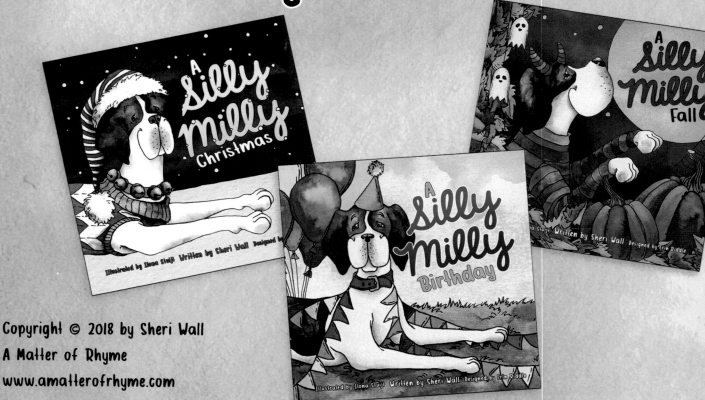

Silly Milly the Dane

Written by Sheri Wall

Illustrated by Ilona Stuijt

Designed by Erin Riddle

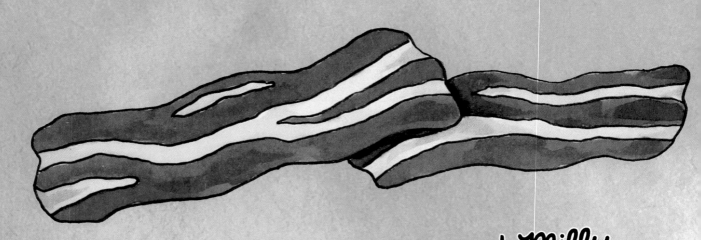

I have a Great Dane named Milly

She frolics and woofs willy-nilly!

She begs for my food

With sad-eyed attitude

Oh Milly, why are you so silly?

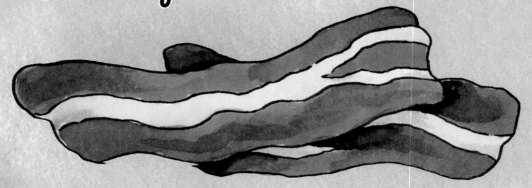

I have a *Great Dane* named *Milly*

She wiggles and yaps *willy-nilly!*

She slobbers and drools

Now I'm all wet too

Oh *Milly,* why are you so *silly?*

I have a Great Dane named Milly
She shimmies and howls willy-nilly!
She wears curtains draped
Down her back as a cape
Oh Milly, why are you so silly?

I have a *Great Dane* named *Milly*

She frolics and woofs willy-nilly!

She won't fetch a stick

But a tree limb she'll pick

Oh *Milly*, why are you so *silly?*

I have a Great Dane named Milly
She wiggles and yaps willy-nilly!
A cushion gets torn
Feathers dancing airborne
Oh Milly, why are you so silly?

I have a Great Dane named Milly
She shimmies and howls willy-nilly!
In the closet she hides
Behind shelves to surprise
Oh Milly, why are you so silly?

I have a *Great Dane* named *Milly*

She frolics and woofs willy-nilly!

She chews my new purse

Now what could be worse

Oh *Milly*, why are you so *silly?*

I have a Great Dane named Milly
She wiggles and yaps willy-nilly!
Squirrels tease her to race
She ends up in last place
Oh Milly, why are you so silly?

I have a *Great Dane* named *Milly*

She shimmies and howls willy-nilly!

You can look but don't touch

Her toy doughnut that's stuffed

Oh *Milly*, why are you so *silly*?

I have a *Great Dane* named *Milly*

She frolics and woofs willy-nilly!

I laugh at her mug

As she twirls on the rug

Oh *Milly*, why are you so *silly?*

I have a *Great Dane* named *Milly*

She wiggles and yaps willy-nilly!

Barking when she can see

Her new friend on TV

Oh *Milly*, why are you so *silly?*

I have a Great Dane named Milly
She shimmies and howls willy-nilly!
Paws wave overhead
As she naps in her bed
Oh Milly, why are you so silly?

I have a *Great Dane* named *Milly*
She frolics and woofs willy-nilly!
Being lazy all day
From my side she won't stray
Oh *Milly*, why are you so *silly*?

I have a *Great Dane* named *Milly*

She wiggles and yaps *willy-nilly!*

I snap a close-up

Of my warm, snuggly pup

Oh *Milly*, why are you so *silly?*

I have a *Great Dane* named *Milly*

She shimmies and howls *willy-nilly!*

She's the very best pet

In the world I would bet

My *Milly,* I love you so *silly!*

Sheri Wall is a wife, mom, Great Dane aunt, Texan, and an award-winning children's book author. She uses rhymes and repetitive verse as essential learning tools in her writings. Sheri enjoys cooking, eating, decorating, bargain hunting, and being active. See more of Sheri's books at amatterofrhyme.com.

Ilona Stuijt is a Dutch illustrator who has worked on children's books and a variety of other artistic projects all over the world. You can find her illustrations and creative works at lankyartist.com.

Erin Riddle is a vintage-style photographer at Lone Star Pin-up and Vintage Luxe in Texas. In addition to loving Great Danes, she also enjoys singing, shopping, and spending time with friends and family. She is beyond excited to share a little silliness with everyone through her lovable stinkmuffin, Milly.

Made in the USA
Las Vegas, NV
09 November 2021